DISABILITY AND FAMILIES

Families Today

Adoptive Families

Disability and Families

Foster Families

Homelessness and Families

Immigrant Families

Incarceration and Families

LGBT Families

Military Families

Multigenerational Families

Multiracial Families

Single-Parent Families

Teen Parents

Families Today

DISABILITY AND FAMILIES

H.W. Poole

MASON CREST

Mason Crest
450 Parkway Drive, Suite D
Broomall, PA 19008
www.masoncrest.com

MTM Publishing, Inc.
435 West 23rd Street, #8C
New York, NY 10011
www.mtmpublishing.com

President: Valerie Tomaselli
Vice President, Book Development: Hilary Poole
Designer: Annemarie Redmond
Copyeditor: Peter Jaskowiak
Editorial Assistant: Andrea St. Aubin

Series ISBN: 978-1-4222-3612-3
Hardback ISBN: 978-1-4222-3614-7
E-Book ISBN: 978-1-4222-8258-8

Library of Congress Cataloging-in-Publication Data
Names: Poole, Hilary W., author.
Title: Disability and families / by H.W. Poole.
Description: Broomall, PA : Mason Crest [2017] | Series: Families Today | Includes index.
Identifiers: LCCN 2016004549| ISBN 9781422236147 (hardback) | ISBN 9781422236123
(series) | ISBN 9781422282588 (e-book)
Subjects: LCSH: People with disabilities—Family relationships—Juvenile literature.
| Parents with disabilities—Juvenile literature. | Children with disabilities—Juvenile
literature. | Families—Juvenile literature.
Classification: LCC HV1568 .P66 2017 | DDC 362.4/043—dc23
LC record available at http://lccn.loc.gov/2016004549

Printed and bound in the United States of America.

First printing
9 8 7 6 5 4 3 2 1

TABLE OF CONTENTS

Series Introduction 7

Chapter One: What Is Disability?. 11

Chapter Two: Physical Challenges 19

Chapter Three: Cognitive Challenges. 27

Chapter Four: Disability in Your Family. 37

Further Reading 44

Series Glossary 45

Index 47

About the Author 48

Photo Credits 48

Key Icons to Look for:

Words to Understand: These words with their easy-to-understand definitions will increase the reader's understanding of the text, while building vocabulary skills.

Sidebars: This boxed material within the main text allows readers to build knowledge, gain insights, explore possibilities, and broaden their perspectives by weaving together additional information to provide realistic and holistic perspectives.

Research Projects: Readers are pointed toward areas of further inquiry connected to each chapter. Suggestions are provided for projects that encourage deeper research and analysis.

Text-Dependent Questions: These questions send the reader back to the text for more careful attention to the evidence presented there.

Series Glossary of Key Terms: This back-of-the-book glossary contains terminology used throughout the series. Words found here increase the reader's ability to read and comprehend higher-level books and articles in this field.

In the 21st century, families are more diverse than ever before.

SERIES INTRODUCTION

Our vision of "the traditional family" is not nearly as time-honored as one might think. The standard of a mom, a dad, and a couple of kids in a nice house with a white-picket fence is a relic of the 1950s—the heart of the baby boom era. The tumult of the Great Depression followed by a global war caused many Americans to long for safety and predictability—whether such stability was real or not. A newborn mass media was more than happy to serve up this image, in the form of TV shows like *Leave It To Beaver* and *The Adventures of Ozzie and Harriet*. Interestingly, even back in the "glory days" of the traditional family, things were never as simple as they seemed. For example, a number of the classic "traditional" family shows— such as *The Andy Griffith Show, My Three Sons,* and a bit later, *The Courtship of Eddie's Father*—were actually focused on single-parent families.

Sure enough, by the 1960s our image of the "perfect family" was already beginning to fray at the seams. The women's movement, the gay rights movement, and—perhaps more than any single factor—the advent of "no fault" divorce meant that the illusion of the Cleaver family would become harder and harder to maintain. By the early 21st century, only about 7 percent of all family households were traditional—defined as a married couple with children where *only* the father works outside the home.

As the number of these traditional families has declined, "nontraditional" arrangements have increased. There are more single parents, more gay and lesbian parents, and more grandparents raising grandchildren than ever before. Multiracial families—created either through interracial relationships or adoption—are also increasing. Meanwhile, the transition to an all-volunteer military force has meant that there are more kids growing up in military families than there were in the past. Each of these topics is treated in a separate volume in this set.

While some commentators bemoan the decline of the traditional family, others argue that, overall, the recognition of new family arrangements has brought more good than bad. After all, if very few people live like the Cleavers anyway, isn't it better to be honest about that fact? Surely, holding up the traditional family as an ideal to which all should aspire only serves to stigmatize kids whose lives differ from that standard. After all, no children can be held responsible for whatever family they find themselves in; all they can do is grow up as best they can. These books take the position that every family—no matter what it looks like—has the potential to be a successful family.

That being said, challenges and difficulties arise in every family, and nontraditional ones are no exception. For example, single parents tend to be less well off financially than married parents are, and this has long-term impacts on their children. Meanwhile, teenagers who become parents tend to let their educations suffer, which damages their income potential and career possibilities, as well as risking the future educational attainment of their babies. There are some 400,000 children in the foster care system at any given time. We know that the uncertainty of foster care creates real challenges when it comes to both education and emotional health.

Furthermore, some types of "nontraditional" families are ones we wish did not have to exist at all. For example, an estimated 1.6 million children experience homelessness at some point in their lives. At least 40 percent of homeless kids are lesbian, gay, bisexual, or transgender teens who were turned out of their homes because of their orientation. Meanwhile, the United States incarcerates more people than any other nation in the world—about 2.7 million kids (1 in 28) have an incarcerated parent. It would be absurd to pretend that such situations are not extremely stressful and, often, detrimental to kids who have to survive them.

The goal of this set, then, is twofold. First, we've tried to describe the history and shape of various nontraditional families in such a way that kids who aren't familiar with them will be able to not only understand, but empathize. We also present demographic information that may be useful for students who are dipping their toes into introductory sociology concepts.

Second, we have tried to speak specifically to the young people who are living in these nontraditional families. The series strives to address these kids as

Meeting challenges and overcoming them together can make families stronger.

sympathetically and supportively as possible. The volumes look at some of the typical problems that kids in these situations face, and where appropriate, they offer advice and tips for how these kids might get along better in whatever situation confronts them.

Obviously, no single book—whether on disability, the military, divorce, or some other topic—can hope to answer every question or address every problem. To that end, a "Further Reading" section at the back of each book attempts to offer some places to look next. We have also listed appropriate crisis hotlines, for anyone with a need more immediate than can be addressed by a library.

Whether your students have a project to complete or a problem to solve, we hope they will be able to find clear, empathic information about nontraditional families in these pages.

—H. W. Poole

Parents all have dreams for how their children's lives will turn out, and it can be hard when things don't go according to plan.

Chapter One

WHAT IS DISABILITY?

Humans are unique among animals because we make plans and dream about the future. Whether it's tomorrow or next month or years from now, we all have ideas about how things are going to go. This is especially true for parents looking forward to the birth of a baby. Months are spent joyfully waiting for the new family member's arrival. Frequently, the baby arrives healthy and **typical** in all the ways that parents expect their babies to be. Other times, parents discover that their baby has developed in a less typical way.

Sometimes, the wrinkle in our plans comes later, as the result of an accident, an illness, a war, or the like. We wake up one morning to find that life has not turned out as we planned.

Words to Understand

ambulatory: having to do with movement or walking.

cognitive: having to do with thinking or understanding.

impairment: reduction of an ability, such as "visual impairment."

prevalence: how common a particular trait is in a group of people.

typical: average.

Having a disability may mean that there are certain things you can't do, but you might be surprised at how many things you actually *can* do.

UNDERSTANDING DISABILITY

A disability is sometimes defined as "the inability to move, perceive the world, or think the way others do." The Americans with Disabilities Act of 1990 defines a person as disabled if he or she "has a physical or mental **impairment** that substantially limits one or more major life activities." But what does that really mean?

Let's look at the word *disability* itself. The prefix *dis* comes from Latin, and it means "away" or "apart." And the word *ability* means simply having the means or skill to do a particular thing. So *disability* means the absence of a particular skill. That's an important thing to understand: if we say that a person has a *disability*, we are not saying that person is less worthy than anyone else. Literally, all we are saying is that he or she does not have a specific skill.

There are many, many types of disability. Some can be seen easily. If someone needs a wheelchair or guide dog to get around, that person's disability will be obvious. But many disabilities cannot be seen so easily—sometimes, you won't even know someone has a disability unless he or she tells you.

U.S. government agencies group disabilities into six main types:

- **Hearing,** meaning that the person is either deaf or has a great deal of trouble hearing.
- **Visual,** meaning that the person is either blind or has a great deal of trouble seeing.
- **Cognitive,** meaning that person has a lot of trouble concentrating, learning, remembering, or making decisions.
- **Ambulatory,** meaning that the person has a lot of trouble walking.
- **Self-care,** meaning that the person has a lot of trouble getting dressed, taking baths or showers, or performing other basic tasks to look after himself or herself.
- **Independent living,** meaning that the person has a lot of trouble with things like grocery shopping or getting to doctor's appointments—things that are usually expected of adults who live on their own.

In addition to these six categories, the disabilities that veterans experience are sometimes considered separately. A veteran might have any of the six types of disabilities, or several of them at the same time. But because of the way in which veterans became disabled—that is, on the battlefield—some experts like to consider veterans as a separate group from those who were disabled at birth or who acquired a disability due to illness or accident.

According to the U.S. census, about 19 percent of Americans have some form of disability—that's about

braille alphabet

a b c d e f g h i

j k l m n o p q r

s t u v w x y z

Braille is a system invented in 1824 to make it possible for visually impaired people to read.

56.7 million people, or almost 1 in every 5 Americans. But these are just averages. Disability rates vary a lot depending on age. The 2013 Disability Status Report states that the **prevalence** of disability looks like this:

- age 4 and under: 0.8 percent
- age 5 to 15: 5.3 percent
- age 16 to 20: 5.6 percent
- age 21 to 64: 10.8 percent
- age 65 to 74: 25.8 percent
- age 75 and up: 50.7 percent.

As you can see, most people with disabilities are elderly. And if you look at the categories that list school-age people, you'll see that just over 5 percent have some form of disability. Of course, while 5 percent might *sound* small, it's actually millions of kids.

HOW DOES DISABILITY CHANGE A FAMILY?

The above statistics give us a general picture about who people with disabilities are. But disability doesn't just happen to an individual—it happens to an entire family. If a child has a disability, that child's parents, siblings, and even extended

Disability Statistics

The 2013 Disability Status Report lists the prevalence of each type of disability among the U.S. population:

- visual disability: 2.3 percent
- hearing disability: 3.5 percent
- ambulatory disability: 7.1 percent
- cognitive disability: 5.1 percent
- self-care disability: 2.7 percent
- independent living: 5.6 percent

(Note: The independent living category was only studied with regard to people aged 16 and older; children under the age of 5 were only asked about vision and hearing.)

A disability will change a family, but it can also make them stronger.

family (aunts and uncles, cousins, and grandparents) are all affected in one way or another. And if a parent has a disability, the other parent is affected as well as their children. Unlike an illness, most disabilities do not "go away"—they will be a permanent part of the family's life.

Because there are so many types of disabilities, it is impossible to generalize about how disabilities affect a family. If a parent is deaf, for example, that certainly makes the family different from the "average" family. But does the experience of having a deaf parent create a huge crisis for the rest of the family? Very unlikely. Daily life may be different from what it is for typical families, but a family with a deaf parent will mostly carry on just like anybody else. On the other hand, if, let's say, a car accident causes a family member to be severely disabled, this may create big challenges.

There are usually extra costs related to caring for a person with a disability. Those costs could be fairly low, or they could be very high—a lot depends on the type of disability. For example, if a child has a visual **impairment**, parents might

If a member of your family is hearing impaired, you might learn sign language so that you can communicate better.

have to make changes to their home so that the child can move around safely. If a child has an **ambulatory** disability, the parents will probably have to install ramps and other measures to help their child get around. A child with a **cognitive** impairment might need speech therapy or other tutoring. In fact, a whole team of people might be involved, including physical therapists, doctors or nurses, dietitians, social workers, and so on. All this takes a lot of time and effort, as well as money. It's common for parents to feel drained at times, both financially and emotionally.

Each family member will have to make adjustments. Parents might have to rethink their career goals, because caring for their child takes priority over work. Siblings might feel left out at times. Because so much attention is given to the child with the disability, the rest of the kids might sometimes feel like they are not as important as their brother or sister. If there are a lot of doctor bills, the family might have to watch their money very carefully. And the family's relationship with extended family and friends might change. Some people react badly to people with disabilities—they might be judgmental or just afraid—and so they might back away.

However, there is evidence that disability can actually make families stronger. Each member of the family can learn important lessons—about empathy, patience, and loyalty, among other things. Despite all the challenges, research shows that most people who have a family member with a disability do not end up having major emotional problems. Most families adapt and respond to the challenges that a disability brings. Researchers even have a term for this: "family resilience." In fact, many families report that the disability made their family even stronger than before.

Text-Dependent Questions

1. What does the word *disability* actually mean?
2. Name the six main categories of disability.
3. What are some of the impacts that disability might have on a family?

Research Project

Find out more about the Individuals with Disabilities Education Act (IDEA). When was it passed, and what were its intended goals? Find out about how the IDEA is implemented at your school. Do you think the goals of the law have been realized in the day-to-day life of your school?

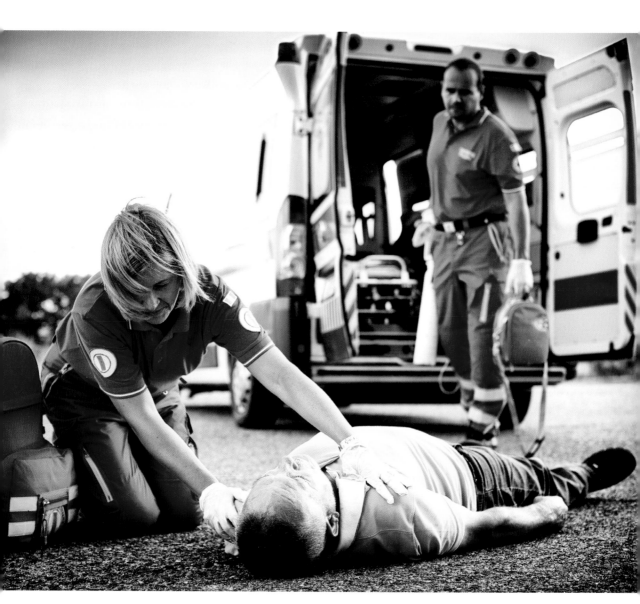

Physical disabilities can be caused by accidents, or they can be present from birth.

Chapter Two

PHYSICAL CHALLENGES

A physical disability means that the person has some kind of challenge that makes it difficult to move in the ways you might expect. One person might use a wheelchair, while someone else might use crutches or a frame to get around. One person might be able to do only certain types of movement, while another person may not be able to move at all.

There are many different reasons a person might have a physical disability. Accidents are one reason. A car accident might cause a spinal injury that prevents the person from walking, for example. Along the same lines, war veterans

Words to Understand

congenital: something a person is born with.

malfunction: not working properly.

orthotics: devices that are used to adjust or assist human movement.

progressive: in this context, something that gets worse over time.

severity: how serious or intense something is.

sometimes have physical disabilities that were caused by gunshots, bombs, or other things that happen in combat. Other physical disabilities are caused by brain injuries or diseases—some that a person has from birth (this is called a **congenital** condition), and some that develop over time. Here are a few common types.

CEREBRAL PALSY

Cerebral palsy (CP) is actually an umbrella term for a few different disorders that all involve having difficulty with movement and balance. But although CP affects movement, the condition actually has nothing to do with the health of the muscles. The disorders are usually caused by an injury to the brain before birth. Most of the time, symptoms of CP are visible by the time a person is three years old. The condition affects 2 to 3 babies out of every 1,000 babies born in the United States.

CP can range from fairly mild, with a small amount of weakness in some parts of the body, to extremely serious, where people are unable to walk or talk and have trouble breathing. Some people with CP have a learning or visual disability as well. Although CP can't be cured, exactly, there is a large range of options available to try and help: surgery, medications, physical therapy, and **orthotics** can all make a huge difference for people with CP. According to the Centers for Disease Control and Prevention (CDC), about 70 percent of people with CP are able to walk—the majority on their own, and some with assistance.

SPINA BIFIDA

Spina bifida is Latin for "split spine," and the condition is a type of neural tube defect. The neural tube is part of an embryo that will become a baby's spine and brain; it develops very early during pregnancy. But sometimes the neural tube does not grow correctly, and this results in spinal problems. Scientists are not completely certain why this happens, but they think that both genetics and nutrition can play a role. This is one reason why pregnant women are advised to take a daily vitamin that is high in folic acid, which plays a key role in cell growth.

Priya Cooper at the 1996 Paralympics. Cooper has cerebral palsy, but it has not stopped her from becoming a highly successful competitive swimmer.

Fiction about Disability

People read nonfiction in order to learn information. But that's not the only type of learning a person can do. Reading fiction can help you learn empathy—the ability to put yourself in someone else's situation and imagine what that person's life might be like. Here are some books involving disability that are recommended by the American Library Association.

Young Readers

Dwight, Laura. *Brothers and Sisters*. New York: Star Bright Books, 2005.

Herrera, Juan Felipe, and Ernesto Cuevas Jr. *Featherless/Desplumado*. New York: Children's Book Press, 2004.

Millman, Isaac. *Moses Goes to a Concert*. New York: Farrar, Straus and Giroux, 1998.

Rabinowitz, Alan, and Cátia Chien. *A Boy and a Jaguar*. Boston: Houghton Mifflin Harcourt, 2014.

Middle-Grade Readers

Fusco, Kimberly Newton. *Tending to Grace*. New York: Knopf, 2004.

Lord, Cynthia. *Rules*. New York: Scholastic Press, 2006.

Martin, Ann M. *Rain Reign*. New York: Feiwel and Friends, 2015.

Palacio, R. J. *Wonder*. New York: Random House, 2012.

Ryan, Pam Muñoz. *Becoming Naomi León*. New York: Scholastic, 2004.

Young Adult Readers

Abeel, Samantha. *My Thirteenth Winter: A Memoir*. New York: Orchard, 2003.

Koertge, Ronald. *Stoner & Spaz*. Somerville, MA: Candlewick Press, 2002.

Giles, Gail. *Girls Like Us*. Somerville, MA: Candlewick, 2014.

Sachar, Louis. *Small Steps*. New York: Delacorte Press, 2006.

Sonnenblick, Jordan. *After Ever After.* New York: Scholastic, 2010.

Trueman, Terry. *Stuck in Neutral.* New York: HarperCollins, 2000.

Spina bifida can range from very mild cases that cause few or no problems, to severe cases where parts of the spine are actually exposed. People with spina bifida often have weakness in their legs and problems with malformed feet, hips, or backs. Surgery can help people with spina bifida, but it doesn't always completely fix the problem.

MUSCULAR DYSTROPHY

The term *muscular dystrophy* (MD) describes a group of conditions that cause people to have trouble maintaining healthy muscle. Some types of MD appear in kids, while others are not visible until adulthood. Weak muscles interfere with movement and, in severe cases, make breathing difficult. Muscular dystrophy is a **progressive** disease. Fortunately, treatments and medications can slow down MD.

OTHER PHYSICAL DISABILITIES

A *stroke* occurs when the brain is deprived of oxygen, either because a blood clot stops oxygen from getting to the brain, or because a blood vessel in the brain **malfunctions**. Lack of oxygen causes brain cells to die. Strokes can interfere with speech, memory, and movement.

Osteogenesis imperfecta (OI) is a condition in which bones break extremely easily. In addition to impaired movement, people with OI may have hearing and/or breathing problems and curved spines.

Spinal cord injuries, or damage to the spinal cord, can result in two types of physical disability: *paraplegia* and *tetraplegia* (also called *quadriplegia*). Paraplegia only affects the lower limbs, or legs; someone with this disability will need a wheelchair to get around, but will have full use of his or her arms. People with tetraplegia have no use of their arms or legs and usually need a lot of assistance to perform day-to-day tasks.

Poliomyelitis, or *polio*, was once every parent's nightmare. Unlike the other conditions on this list, polio is an *infectious* disease of the brain and spinal cord.

It causes severe and incurable weakness in the entire body. As many as 20,000 Americans were paralyzed by polio every year until a vaccine was invented in the 1950s. The disease is still a problem in certain countries, including Pakistan, Nigeria, and Afghanistan.

Hearing and Visual Impairments

As noted in chapter one, disabilities that involve the ears and eyes are usually treated in their own categories; they are not ambulatory disabilities, and they are not cognitive. (They are only discussed here in the "physical challenges" chapter due to the space limitations of this book.)

The eyes and ears work together with the brain to translate images and sounds into meaningful information. When some part of that process does not work, the result can be a visual or hearing impairment. When we think of someone with this type of disability, we tend to think immediately of blindness or deafness. But this is an oversimplification. There are actually many levels of **severity**—in other words, a person doesn't have to be completely blind to be considered visually impaired. You can also be hearing impaired without being completely deaf. There is also a huge range of causes for these impairments. A person could have had the impairment since birth, or he or she could have acquired the disability due to illness or accident.

Both visual and hearing impairments are pretty common disabilities for kids to have. In 2013, it was estimated that almost 700,000 people under age 20 had a visual impairment of some form. Meanwhile, 2 or 3 babies out of every 1,000 are born with noticeable hearing loss. However, not all those babies grow up to be deaf, because new treatments are available that can sometimes restore at least some level of hearing.

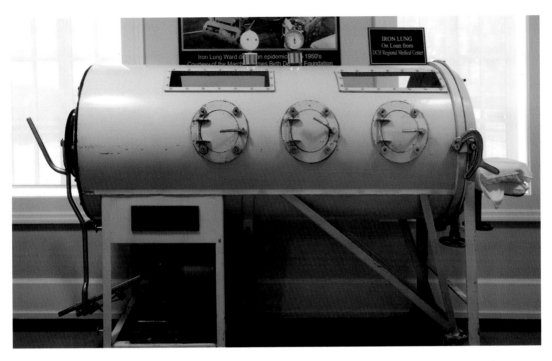

An iron lung from the 1930s. This machine would enable polio patients to breathe when they could no longer do so on their own.

Text-Dependent Questions

1. Does cerebral palsy affect intelligence?
2. What is muscular dystrophy?
3. Name several disabilities that result from problems with the spine.

Research Project

Choose a disability from this chapter that interests you. Find out about its history—when was it discovered, and by whom? Research the history of how people with this disability have been treated. Finally, list some treatments that are currently used to help people with this condition.

A girl with Down Syndrome and her family.

Chapter Three

COGNITIVE CHALLENGES

The word *cognition* comes from the Latin term *cognoscere*, which means "to get to know." If we say that someone has a cognitive disability, that just means they have trouble with some type of mental task. As with physical disabilities, cognitive disabilities come in all shapes and sizes. They may be inconveniences, or, at the other extreme, they may mean that the person needs constant care.

When a doctor evaluates a patient and determines that something is not functioning as it should, that's called a clinical diagnosis. But a lot of people who work in the disability field believe that a *clinical diagnosis* is an inadequate way of talking about cognitive challenges. They prefer to talk about a *functional*

Words to Understand

chromosome: a structure inside a cell that contains genetic information.

genetics: relating to heredity.

inattention: distraction; not paying attention.

spectrum: range.

traumatic: causing long-term (often permanent) damage.

diagnosis. Instead of focusing on the medical aspects of the disorder, a functional diagnosis looks at the effects the disorder has on a person's life. What abilities does the person have or not have, and what can be done to make that aspect of the person's life better?

There are too many types of possible cognitive disabilities to cover all of them here. This chapter will introduce you to a few of the most common.

DOWN SYNDROME

Down syndrome was named for John Langdon Down, an English doctor who wrote about the syndrome in the 1860s. He identified the general characteristics of the disorder, but the real cause was not known until much later, when scientists got a better understanding of **genetics**.

Down Syndrome occurs in families of all races and ethnicities.

> Every day [my brother] Andy teaches me to never give up. He knows he is different, but he doesn't focus on that. He doesn't give up, and every time I see him having a hard time, I make myself work that much harder . . . I don't know what I would do without Andy. He changed my life. . . . If I had not grown up with him, I would have less understanding, patience, and compassion for people. He shows us that anyone can do anything.
>
> —Megan, whose brother Andy has Down syndrome.
>
> Quoted in Donald J. Meyer, *Views from Our Shoes: Growing Up with a Brother or Sister with Special Needs* (Bethesda, MD: Woodbine House, 1997), p. 89.

Humans have **chromosomes**, which contain the genetic material that makes us who we are. There are usually 23 pairs of these chromosomes. Down syndrome is the result of an additional chromosome (or a portion of one) in the 21st pair. Down syndrome is sometimes called trisomy 21; the prefix *"tri"* means 3, and it refers to that extra genetic material. A French doctor known as Jérôme Lejeune discovered the additional genetic material in 1959.

The extra chromosome has a wide variety of impacts. It can affect physical appearance, intellectual development, and overall health. But people with Down syndrome are all unique—there are typical signs, but not every person with Down syndrome will have every single symptom. There are about 400,000 Americans with Down syndrome; about 6,000 new cases are diagnosed each year.

TRAUMATIC BRAIN INJURY

In one sense, an injury to the brain is like an injury to any other part of the body. Something—be it a fall, a car accident, or some other event—creates enough physical force to bruise, break, or otherwise injure someone's body. These injuries can be mild or severe, fixable or unfixable.

But beyond that basic similarity, brain injuries are extremely different from all other types of physical damage. Our brains are the "communication centers" that control everything we do. The way we think, speak, and react to the outside world is what makes us who we are. When people's brains are injured, they may end up very different from the way they were before. The formal term for this situation, **traumatic** brain injury (TBI), emphasizes how serious the situation is. There are more than 5 million Americans who live with disabilities that were caused by these types of injuries.

It is impossible to say what a "typical" TBI is, because there is such a range of injuries and effects. However, the effects of a mild TBI can include memory loss, vision problems, depression, and confusion. The effects of a severe TBI can include the loss of the ability to speak, hear, see, or move—again, depending on the nature of the injury. There are more than 5 million Americans who live with disabilities that were caused by TBIs.

DYSLEXIA

Dyslexia is a very specific type of disability, called a *learning disability*. Unlike other types of cognitive disabilities, which can affect all aspects of someone's life, dyslexia only relates to a person's ability to read. Basically, people with dyslexia have trouble connecting how words sound to how they look when written. Sometimes they may transpose letters or numbers: a person with dyslexia might read "no" as "on," "bed" as "deb," or the number 512 as 152. This very simple challenge can have a huge impact on how people read and, therefore, how they learn.

It's important to understand that dyslexia has nothing to do with how smart someone is. Some of our most brilliant and successful people had dyslexia. Some sources claim that the scientists Albert Einstein and Michael Faraday, inventors

Dyslexia is the most prevalent learning disability in the country; about 20 percent of Americans have dyslexia.

Alexander Graham Bell and Thomas Edison, writers Agatha Christie and F. Scott Fitzgerald, artists Pablo Picasso and Andy Warhol, and filmmakers Walt Disney and Steven Spielberg all had dyslexia.

AUTISM SPECTRUM DISORDERS

Autism is a mental disorder that may affect as many as 1 in 68 kids in the United States. The signs of autism include delays in or difficulty with speech, challenges with communication (understanding facial expressions and gestures), a dislike of being touched or hugged, making repetitive movements or sounds, and extreme reactions to tastes or textures. Not every person with autism has every symptom. As with all the cognitive challenges we've mentioned, autism can range from mild to severe. In fact, that idea is built right into the formal name: autism **spectrum** disorders.

Many people who are "on the spectrum" don't have a disability in the way that, for example, someone who uses a wheelchair does. But remember that the word *disability* just means having difficulty with a particular skill. Autism spectrum disorders also involve problems with particular skills, and that's why they are included as disabilities.

There's also an important practical reason why autism spectrum disorders are called disabilities. If a cognitive challenge meets the legal definition of disability, then that person is eligible for services, and that can make a big difference in his or her life. For example, kids might qualify for extra help at school. People who meet the definition of disability might also be eligible for Social Security, which is an important government safety net. It offers health care and even income support to people who have trouble earning money in traditional ways.

Kids who are on the autism spectrum can really benefit from extra help in class.